How many letters of the alphabet do you know? Say the names of the letters on the alphabet banner. Color the large A.

Skill: introducing the letters of the alphabet

1

Aa

 Place the sticker of the alligator in the box.

 Say the name of each picture. Color the pictures that begin with the same sound as alligator.

astronaut

ant

ball

dog

ambulance

apple

 Trace the letters. Practice printing the letters on the lines.

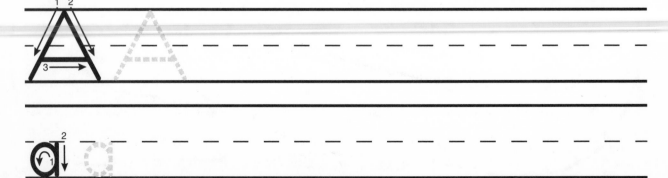

Skill: associating symbols and a sound for the letter A

Color the spaces with the upper or lowercase **Aa** letters in the picture below.

acrobat

Bb

  Place the sticker of the baby in the box.

 Say the name of each picture. Draw a line from **Bb** to each picture that begins with the same sound as baby.

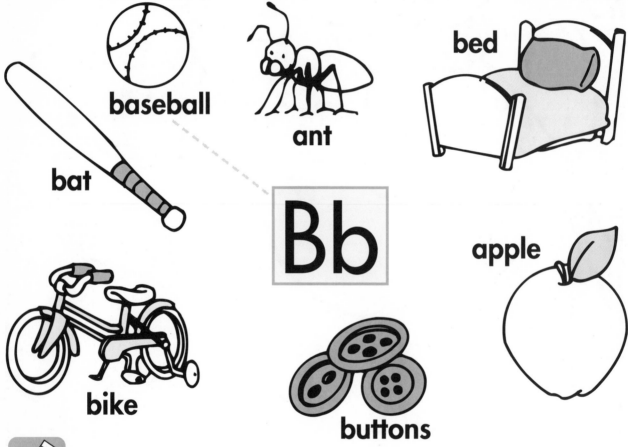

baseball

ant

bed

bat

Bb

apple

bike

buttons

 Trace and write.

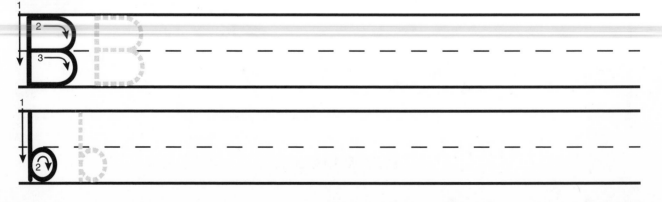

Skill: associating symbols and a sound for the letter B

Banana begins with **Bb**. Draw what you would like to have for breakfast.

Cc

 Place the sticker of the cow in the box.

 Say the name of each picture. Draw a circle around the pictures that begin with the same sound as cow.

comb

bed

car

cat

castle

astronaut

 Trace and write.

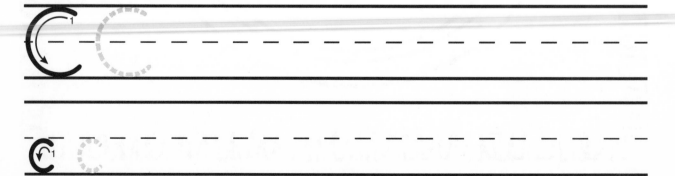

Skill: associating symbols and a sound for the letter C

Follow the path to get the camper to his car.

Dd

 Place the sticker of the dog in the box.

 Say the name of each picture. Color the pictures that begin with the same sound as dog.

comb

dinosaur

ball

desk

duck

doctor

 Trace and write.

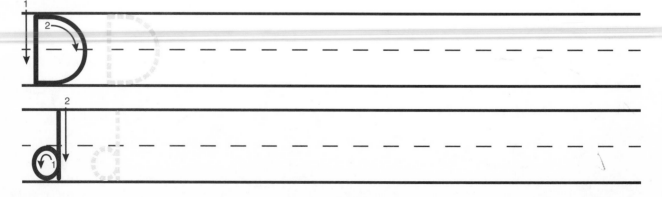

8

Say the name of each picture. Draw lines to match the pictures that begin with the same sound.

Ee

 Place the sticker of the elephant in the box.

 Say the name of each picture. Draw a line from **Ee** to each picture that begins with the same sound as elephant.

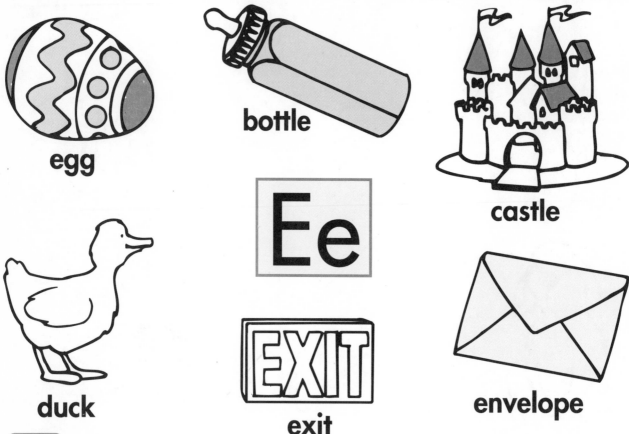

egg

bottle

castle

Ee

duck

exit

envelope

 Trace and write.

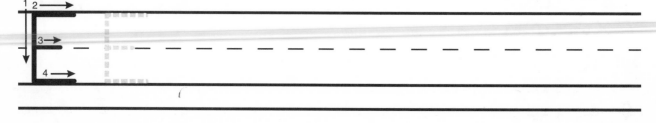

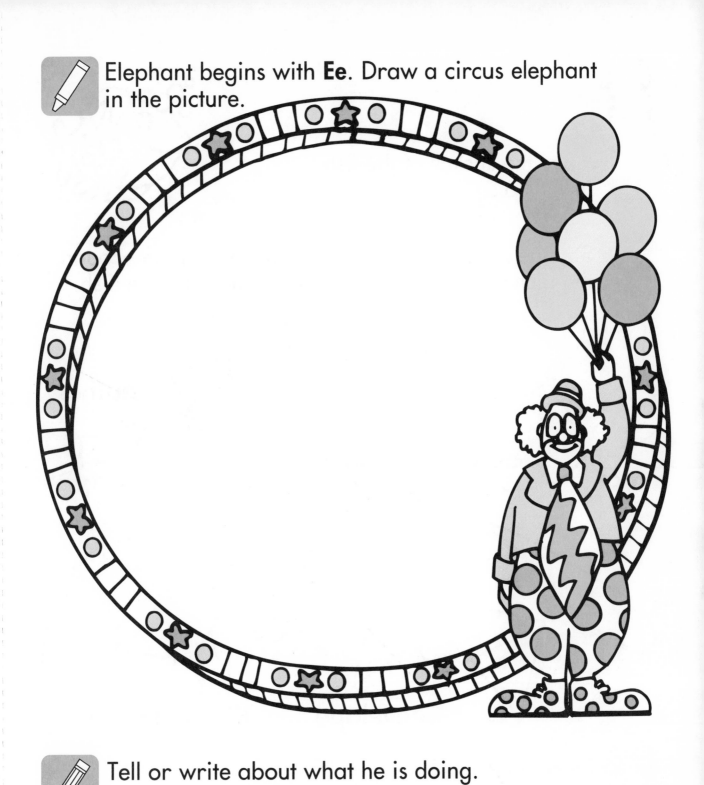

Elephant begins with **Ee**. Draw a circus elephant in the picture.

Tell or write about what he is doing.

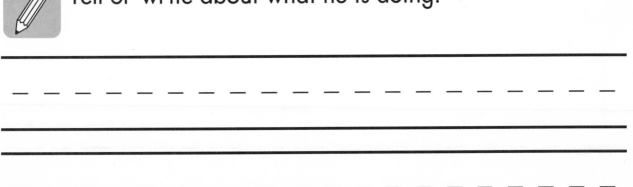

Ff

 Place the sticker of the fish in the box.

 Say the name of each picture. Draw a circle around the pictures that begin with the same sound as fish.

foot

feather

fork

envelope

dinosaur

 Trace and write.

12

Fish begins with **Ff**. Draw fish in the fish tank.

 Name your fish. Tell or write about what they are doing.

Gg

 Place the sticker of the guitar in the box.

 Say the name of each object. Color the objects in the picture that begin with the same sound as guitar.

 Trace and write.

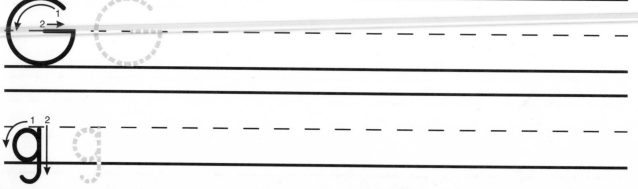

<u>Skill</u>: associating symbols and a sound for the letter G

Color all the upper and lowercase **Gg** letters in the alphabet soup.

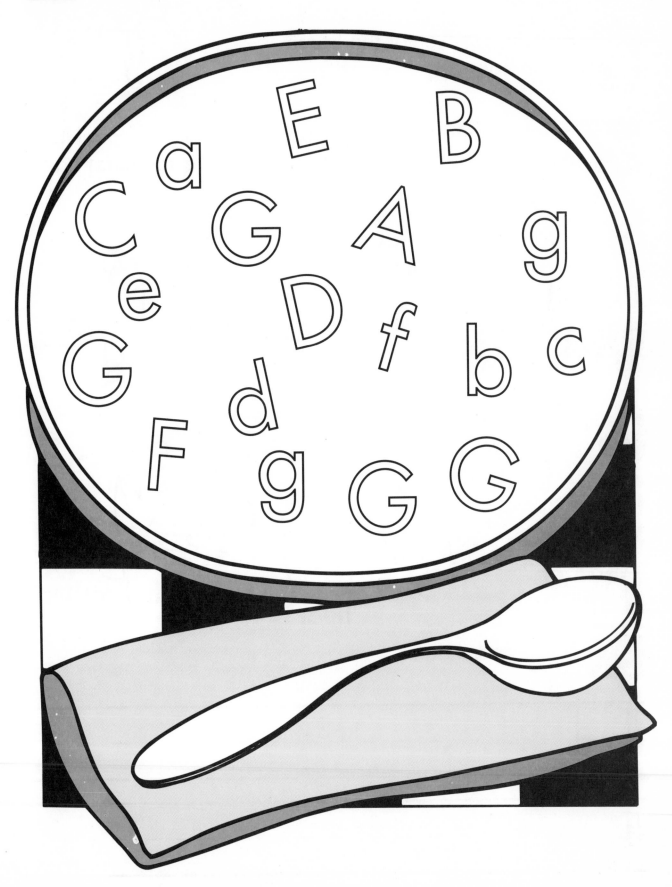

Hh

 Place the sticker of the horse in the box.

 Say the name of each picture. Draw a line from **Hh** to each picture that begins with the same sound as horse.

goat

hat

hammer

Hh

feather

heart

helicopter

 Trace and write.

Skill: associating symbols and a sound for the letter H

Find and circle the objects in the picture that begin with **Hh**. Draw some hay for the horse to eat.

Skill: reinforcing the sound for the letter H

Ii

 Place the sticker of the igloo in the box.

 Say the name of each picture. Color the pictures that begin with the same sound as igloo.

ink

egg

iguana

fish

insect

hammer

Trace and write.

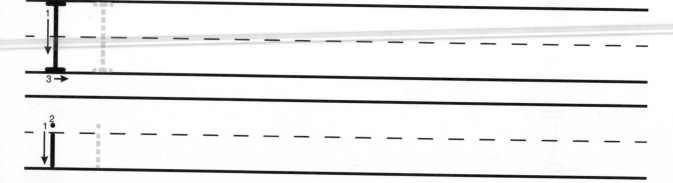

Skill: associating symbols and a sound for the letter I

Draw a line from each picture to the letter that makes the same beginning sound. Write the upper and lowercase letters that make the beginning sound of the picture that is left.

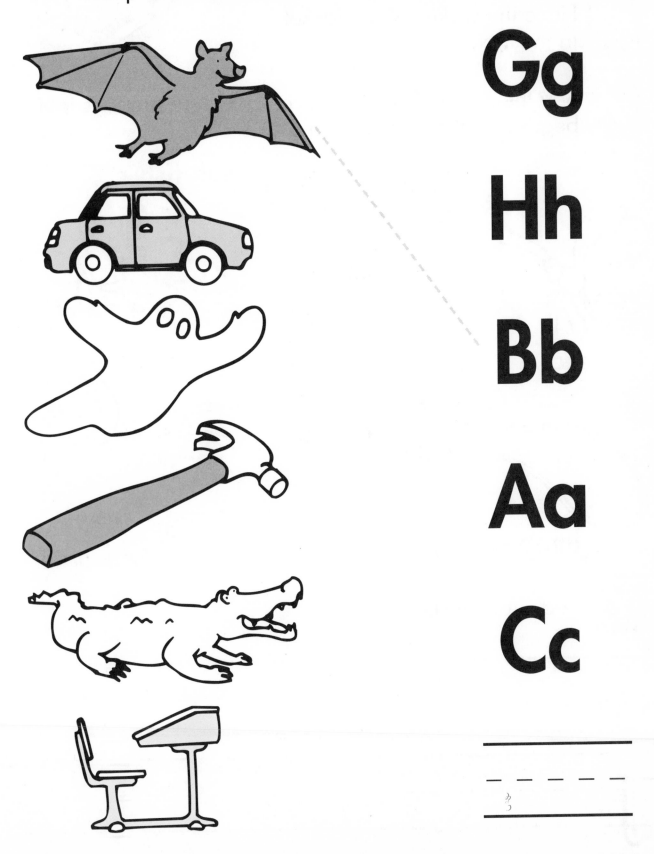

Gg

Hh

Bb

Aa

Cc

Jj

 Place the sticker of the jacket in the box.

 Say the name of each picture. Color the pictures that begin with the same sound as jacket.

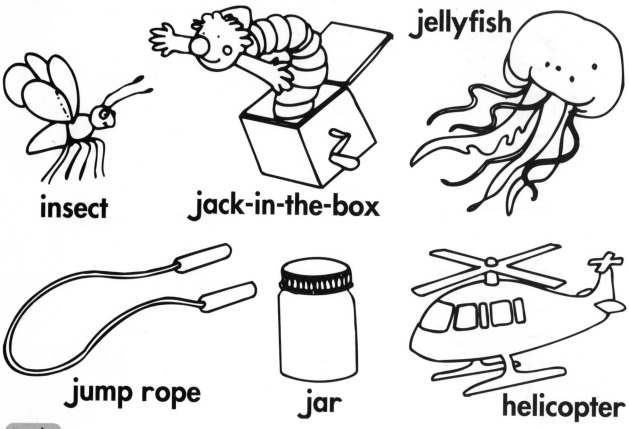

jellyfish

insect

jack-in-the-box

jump rope

jar

helicopter

 Trace and write.

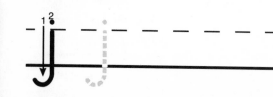

Skill: associating symbols and a sound for the letter J

Find and color all the upper and lowercase **J j** letters that are hidden in the picture.

Kk

Place the sticker of the kangaroo in the box.

Say the name of each picture. Write the letter for the beginning sound under each picture.

Trace and write.

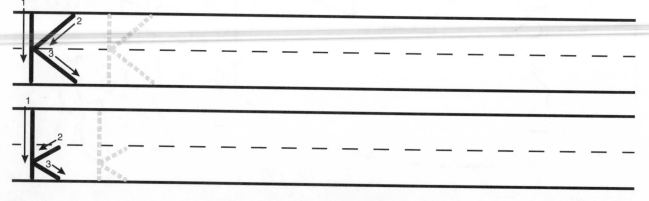

Kite begins with **Kk**. Decorate the kite.

LI

 Place the sticker of the lion
in the box.

 Find the two lions that are the same. Color them.

 Trace and write.

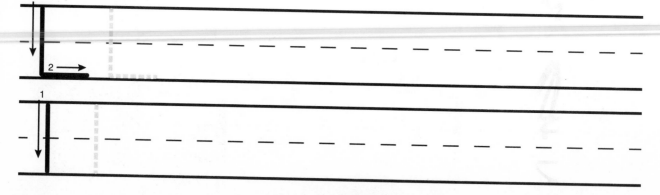

Skill: associating symbols and a sound for the letter L

Draw lines to match the upper and lowercase letters.

A
B
E
F
H
I
J
L

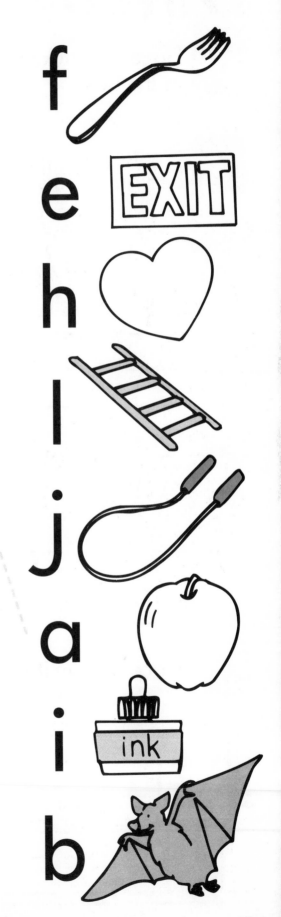

f
e
h
l
j
a
i
b

Mm

 Place the sticker of the monkey in the box.

 Say the name of each picture. Write the letter for the beginning sound under each picture.

_____   _____   _____   _____

- - - - - - - - -   - - - - - - - - -   - - - - - - - - -   - - - - - - - - -

_____   _____   _____   _____

_____   _____   _____   _____

- - - - - - - - -   - - - - - - - - -   - - - - - - - - -   - - - - - - - - -

_____   _____   _____   _____

 Trace and write.

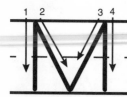

26

Mouse Race

You will need: 1 coin, 2 counters (buttons, stones, etc.), and a partner.

Directions: Flip the coin. Heads moves one space; tails moves two spaces. Say the name of the letter you land on. Try to be the first person to get your mouse to the house.

Nn

 Place the sticker of the nickel in the box.

 Say the name of each picture. Draw a line from **Nn** to each picture that begins with the same sound as nickel.

nurse

lamp

nut

nail

Nn

mouse

nest

necklace

 Trace and write.

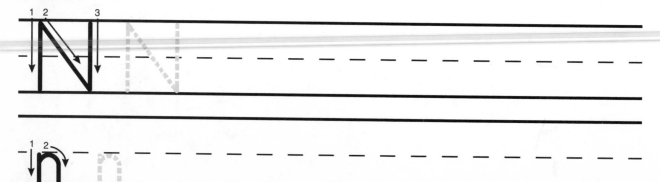

<u>Skill</u>: associating symbols and a sound for the letter N

Circle the lowercase letter that matches the uppercase letter.

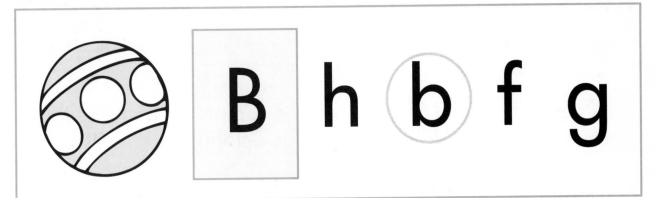

B h (b) f g

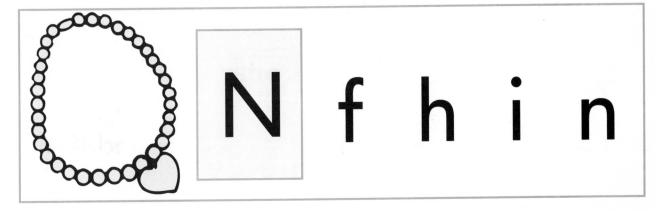

M e m k d

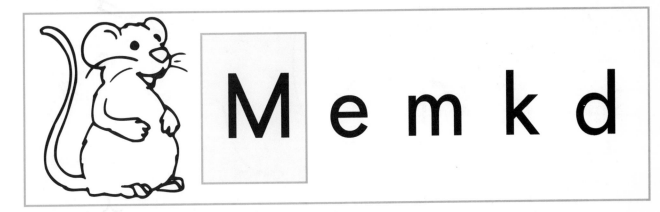

N f h i n

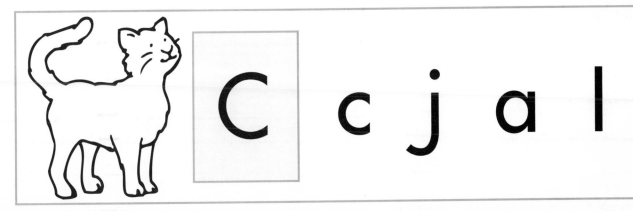

C c j a l

 Place the sticker of the octopus in the box.

 Say the name of each picture. Color the pictures that begin with the same sound as octopus.

monkey

olive

ostrich

otter

octopus

necklace

 Trace and write.

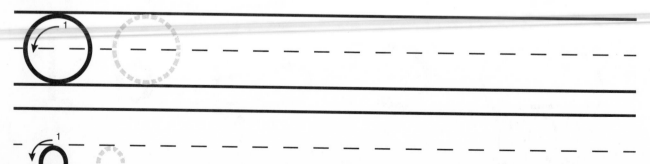

<u>Skill</u>: associating symbols and a sound for the letter O

Color the spaces with the upper or lowercase **Oo** letters in the picture below.

owl

Pp

Place the sticker of the penguin in the box.

Say the name of each picture. Write the letter for the beginning sound under each picture.

Trace and write.

P

p

Picnic starts with **Pp**. Fill the picnic basket with good things to eat.

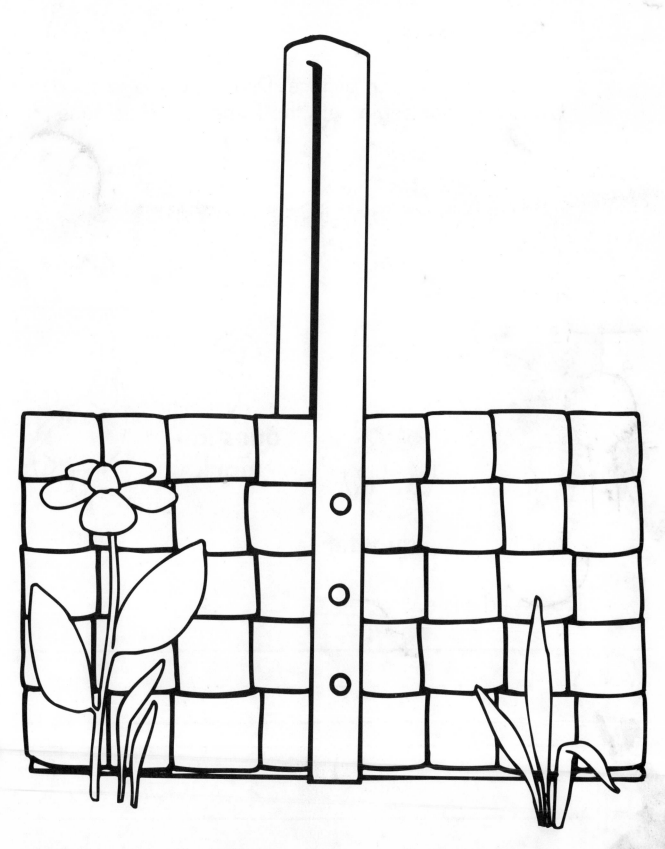

Qq

 Place the sticker of the queen in the box.

 Say the name of each picture. Draw a circle around the pictures that begin with the same sound as queen.

grapes

quilt

monkey

question mark

leaf

quarter

quail

 Trace and write.

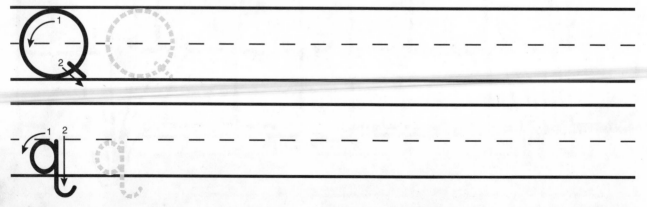

Skill: associating symbols and a sound for the letter Q

Quilt begins with **Qq**. Draw designs to decorate the quilt.

Rr

Place the sticker of the raccoon in the box.

Say the name of each picture. Draw a line from **Rr** to each picture that begins with the same sound as raccoon.

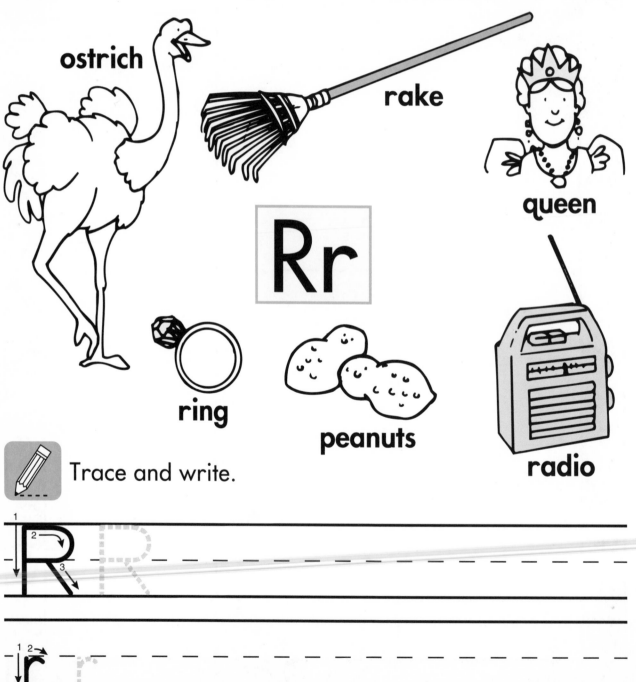

ostrich

rake

queen

Rr

ring

peanuts

radio

Trace and write.

R R

r r

Rainbow begins with **Rr**. Color the rainbow. Add things to your picture.

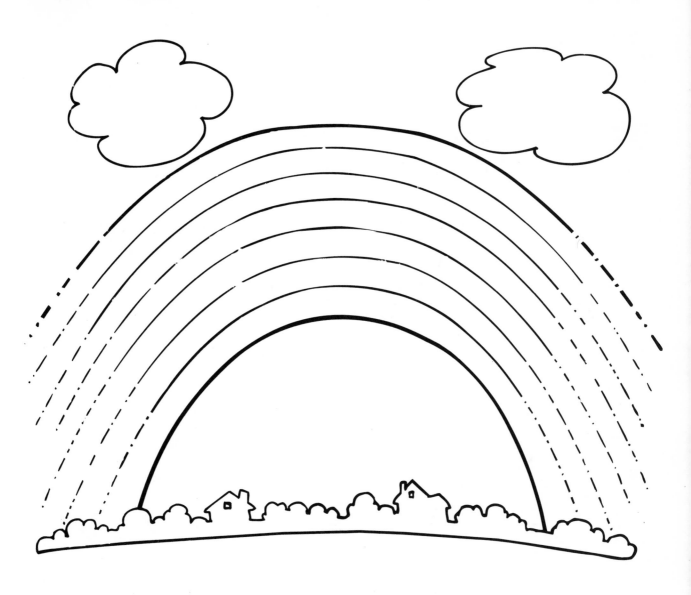

Tell or write about your picture.

_____

- - - - - - - - - - - - - - - - -

_____

- - - - - - - - - - - - - - - - -

_____

Ss

 Place the sticker of the seal in the box.

 Say the name of each picture. Draw a line from **Ss** to each picture that begins with the same sound as seal.

quarter   **soap**   **sink**

Ss

ring

sun   **socks**   **scissors**

 Trace and write.

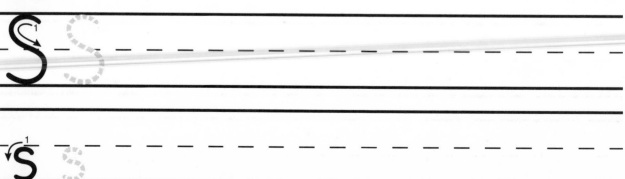

Skill: associating symbols and a sound for the letter S

Fill in the uppercase letters that are missing in the snakes.

Tt

 Place the sticker of the turtle in the box.

 Say the name of each picture. Color the things in the picture that begin with the same sound as turtle.

 Trace and write.

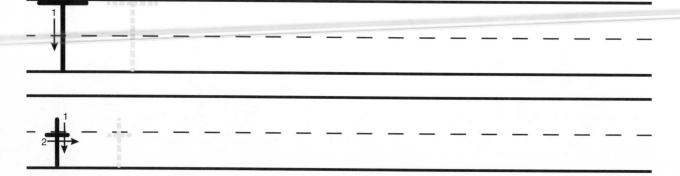

Skill: associating symbols and a sound for the letter T

Add the missing upper and lowercase letters to the train.

Uu

 Place the sticker of the umbrella in the box.

 Color the spaces with the upper or lowercase Uu letters in the picture below.

umpire

Trace and write.

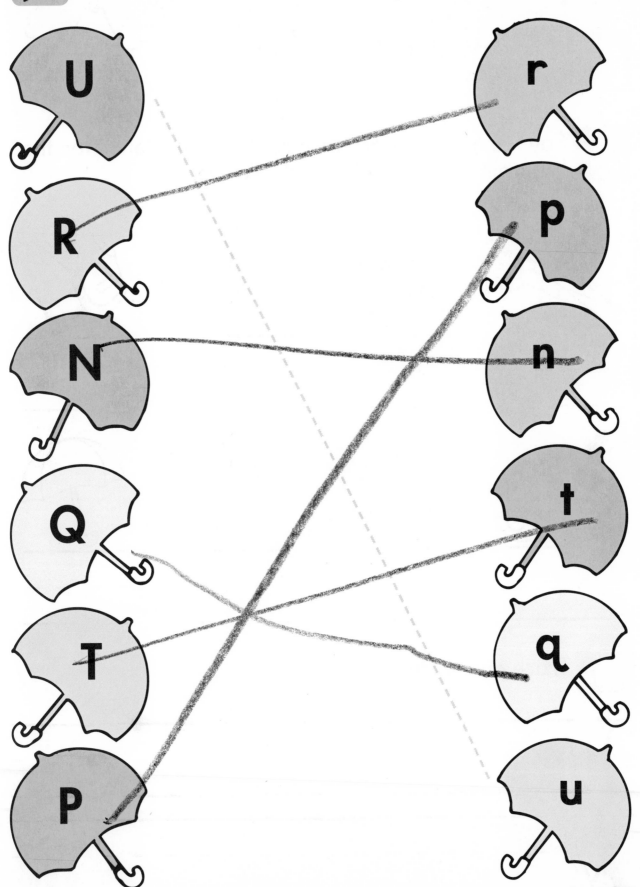

Vv

 Place the sticker of the volcano in the box.

 Say the name of each picture. Write the letter for the beginning sound under each picture.

 Trace and write.

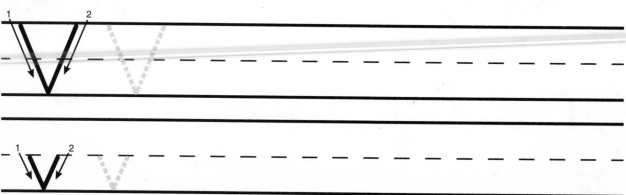

44

Vase begins with **Vv**. Draw some flowers in the vase.

Ww

 Place the sticker of the watch in the box.

 Say the name of each picture. Draw a circle around the pictures that begin with the same sound as watch.

snowman

witch

violin

web

watermelon

worm

wagon

 Trace and write.

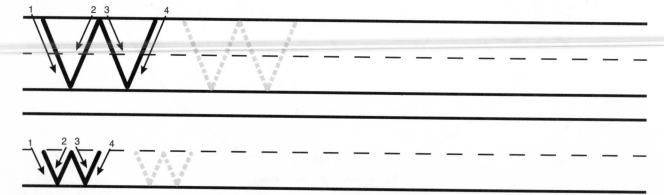

Wagon begins with **Ww**. Fill the wagon with things you like to play with.

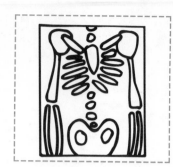

 Place the sticker of the X ray in the box.

 Find and color all the upper and lowercase **Xx** letters that are hidden in the picture.

 Trace and write.

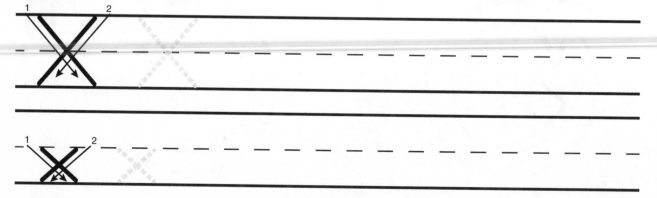

48

Race to the Finish

You will need: 1 coin, 2 counters (buttons, stones, etc.), and a partner.

Directions: Flip the coin. Heads moves one space, tails moves two spaces. Say the name of the letter you land on. Try to be the first person to land on X.

Yy

 Place the sticker of the yo-yo in the box.

 Color the yak. Draw a yellow flower.

 Trace and write.

Yard begins with **Yy**. Draw a picture of what you play with in your yard.

Zz

 Place the sticker of the zebra in the box.

 Say the name of each picture. Color the pictures that begin with the same sound as zebra.

zipper

X ray

zinnia

zebra

wagon

yak

zoo

 Trace and write.

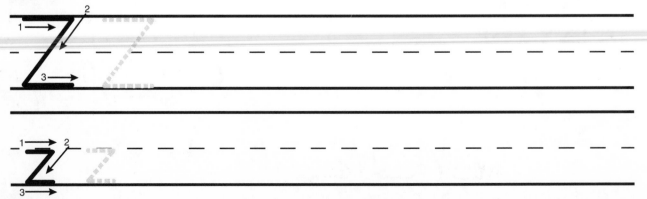

Connect the letters from A to Z. What do you see?

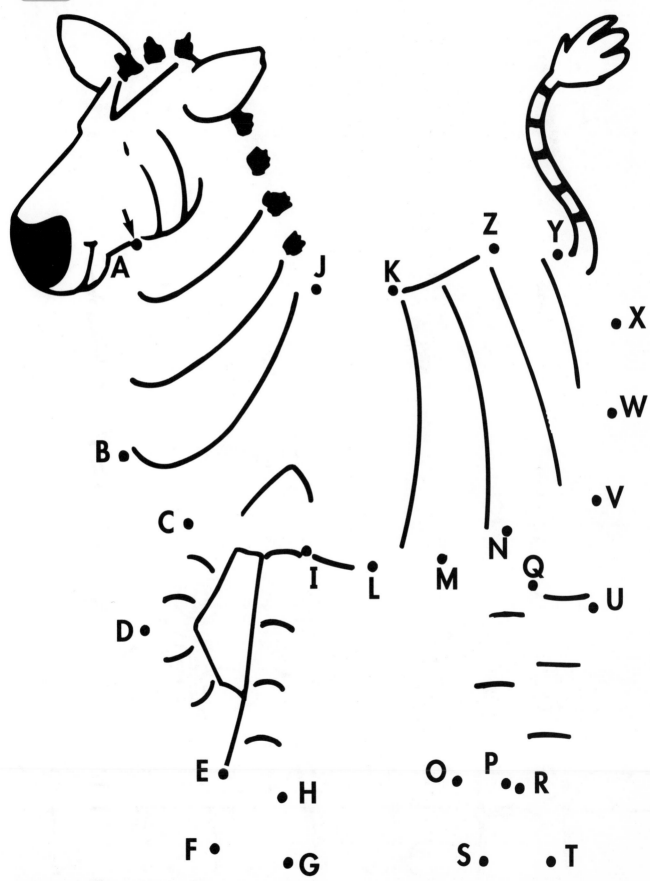

Draw lines to match the uppercase letters in the butterflies to the lowercase letters in the flowers.

54

Alphabet Puzzles

Cut out all the letter squares on the following pages. Match each uppercase letter with its lowercase letter. Turn the cards over to see something that begins with the same sound.

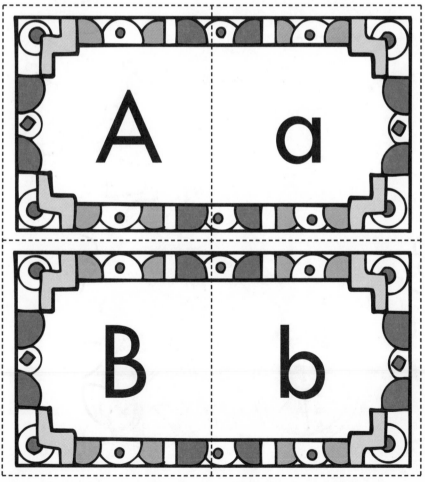

<u>Skill</u>: matching uppercase letters to lowercase letters

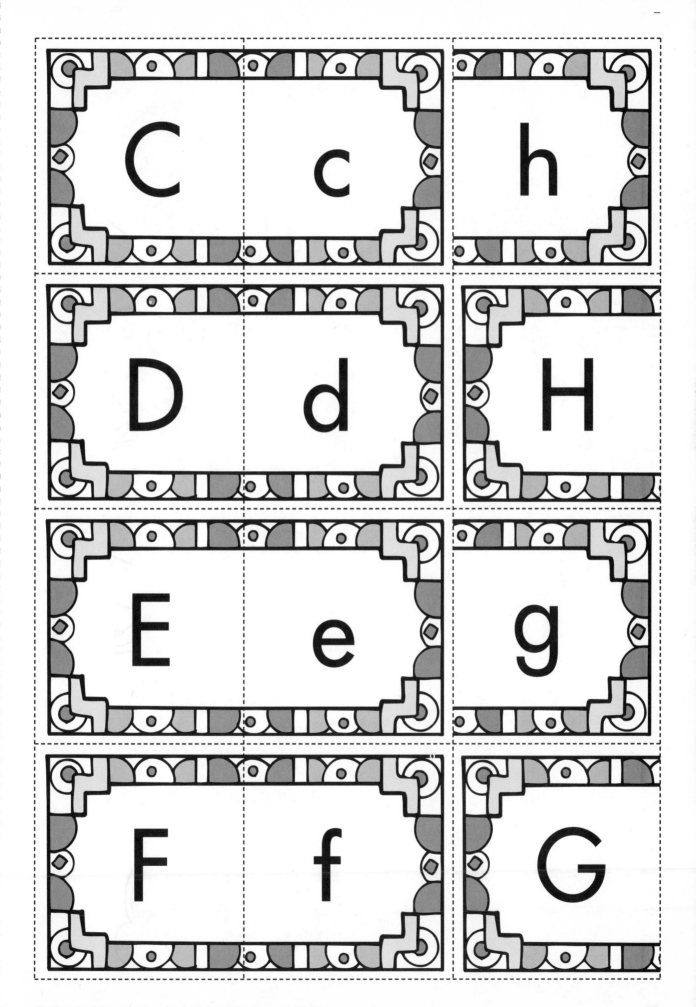

C c

h

D d

H

E e

g

F f

G

<u>Skill:</u> matching uppercase letters to lowercase letters

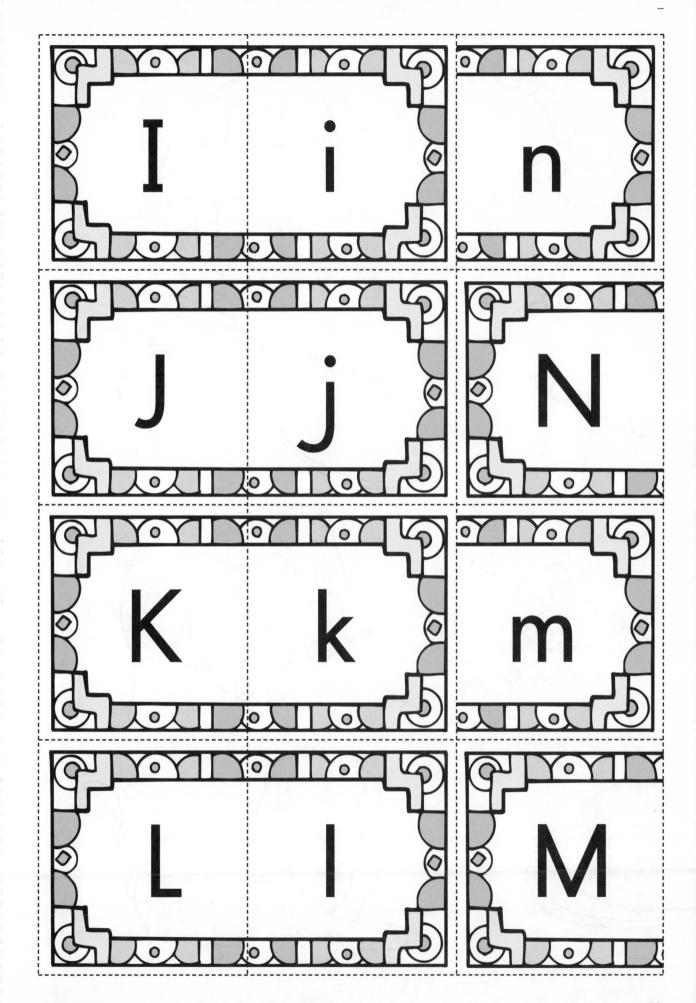

60

Skill: matching uppercase letters to lowercase letters

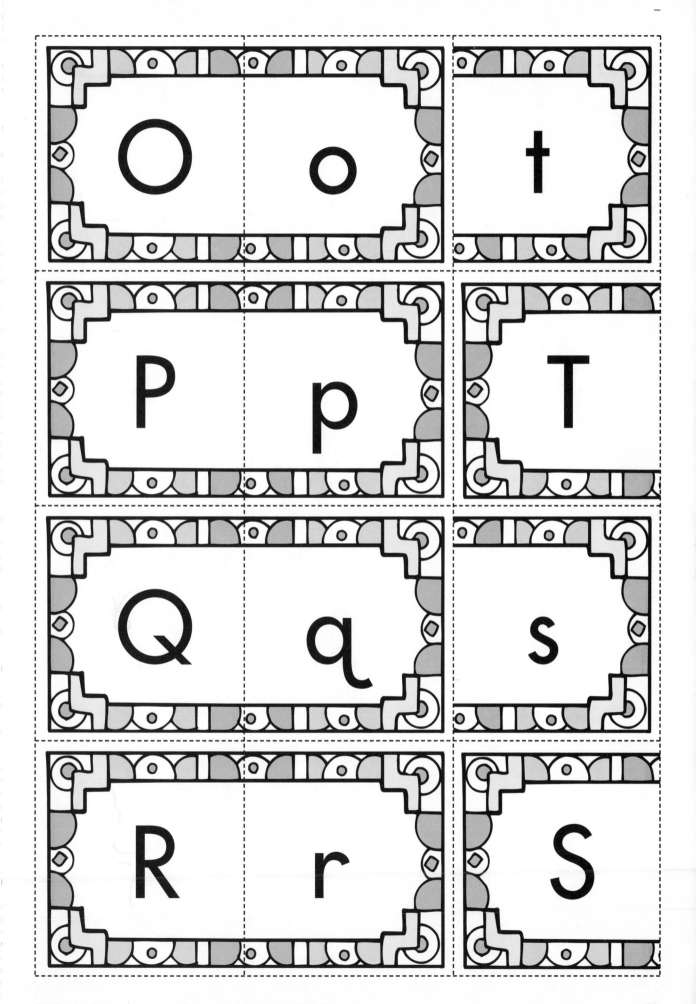

<u>Skill</u>: matching uppercase letters to lowercase letters

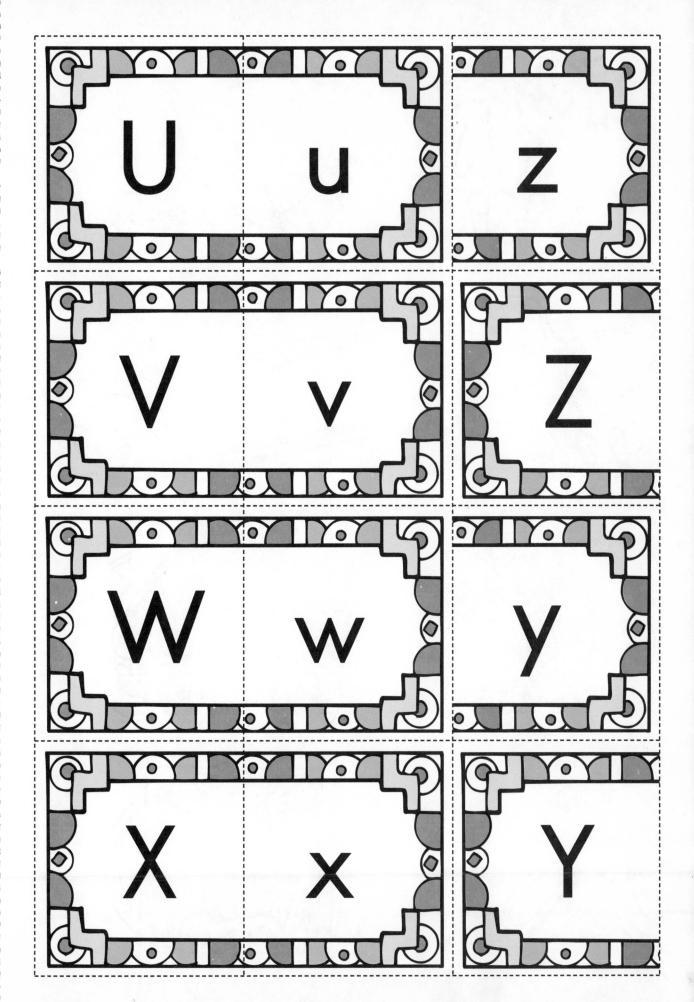

64